THESE
ARE
OUR
BODIES

FOR HIGH SCHOOL

Church Publishing
NEW YORK

PARENT BOOK

Scripture quotations from the CEB used with permission. All rights reserved. Common English Bible, Copyright 2011.

Scripture from the *New Revised Standard Version Bible (NRSV)* © 1989 by the Division of Christian Education of the National Council of Churches of Christ in the USA. Used by permission.

A catalog record of this book is available from the Library of Congress.

Church Publishing Incorporated
19 East 34th Street
New York, NY 10016

Cover design by: Jennifer Kopec, 2 Pug Design
Typeset by: Progressive Publishing Services

ISBN-13: 978-1-60674-331-7 (pbk.)
ISBN-13: 978-1-60674-332-4 (ebook)

Printed in the United States of America

CONTENTS

INTRODUCTION

Welcome to *These Are Our Bodies*!

We are so glad that you and your child are participating in this program and that you have this *Parent Book*. This book is your guide to use alongside each session your child attends.

These Are Our Bodies is about connecting your faith life with your sexuality . . . this is very important and often unexplored territory. This book will help you follow what your child is learning throughout the program and equip you to have conversations related to the topics covered. The book provides prayers, Scripture references, and reflection questions designed to help you see the connection between sexuality and faith. We suggest using the New Revised Standard Version (NRSV) or Common English Bible (CEB) as the Bible version for your Scripture reading.

By the end of the program you will have the tools you need to articulate your own Theology of Sexuality and to have discussions about sexuality with your child. As you take a critical look at the nature of God (theology) and relate it to emotional, physical, and social well-being when it comes to matters of sex and sexuality, we hope you can better discern the ways in which God is calling each of us to be sexual spiritual beings. We encourage you to find the intersection of your sexual expression and your Christian faith for yourself and then to help your child do so as well. As the primary sexuality educator of your child, you are an integral part of the program.

About the Program

The program is a developmentally appropriate and a faith-based approach to sexuality that invites you to explore human sexuality in the context of faith. At the core of each session, framed and informed by Scripture, are concepts such as God's creation, covenant, sexuality as a gift from God, identity, and relationships. Conversations and hands-on activities engage teens in deepening their understanding of self, others, behavior, language, and God's grace and love for them.

Young people in middle adolescence (ages 15–18) and late adolescence (ages 17–19) are gaining a more complex sense of self and their identity. This includes their sexual identity, behaviors, peer relationships, and emotions. As with all adolescents, high school age youth need reassurance from parents, teachers, and mentors that their growth and development is normal. At this time in their life they are looking beyond home and family toward independence, college or a career, the possibility of long-term relationships, and so much more. While growing into a firmer individual identity, the role of family and a faith community continue to be important during these years. They continue to need trusted people who can be a sounding board for their ideas, interests, and problems. Adult mentors have an important role in helping older adolescents solidify a moral code of personal behavior and healthy life practices. In addition to discussing how sexuality is a gift from God, that is what this program is about.

High schoolers experience a challenging phase of life where their bodies are almost fully formed: they look like adults, and are often treated as such, yet they don't have the decision-making skills (or brain power) to react in an adult manner. These years of personality development usually involve separating themselves from their parents by trying on different ideologies, fashions, and decision-making styles. As youth move away from their families as their primary support system, church youth groups can provide a stable, loving group of peers and mentors in which to test their independence. The sessions in *These Are Our Bodies for High School* explore all the aspects of growing into responsible, respectful, Christian adults while giving participants skills to survive high school. In conversations about real-world scenarios, discussions of Scripture, and times of prayer together, the group will safely discern the intersection of their sexuality and spirituality. Leaders will model relationship skills such as listening, empathy, and problem solving as they explore topics with the group and answer questions in an open and healthy atmosphere.

You might notice that we use "our" for the main pronoun throughout this program. Although teenagers are building their own autonomy, individuality, and independence, when it comes to things we struggle with it is comforting to know that we are not alone. As a community that supports each other, challenges each other, and loves each other, we share so much in common. Helping teens learn to feel and receive empathy will guide them to become adult Christians who have healthy relationships and solid self-esteem.

Within these sessions there is an assumption that high school students (for the most part) are nearly through or have completed puberty. While growth spurts may continue, they are beginning to be more comfortable with their bodies and the changes they have physically undergone in recent years. Their focus is now on building stronger relationships and bonds with others, experimentation around identity, relationships, and their sexuality, and what the future may hold upon completion of high school. It is about where they fit in the greater world as an emerging adult, including their sexuality.

All of this is grounded in our faith. *These Are Our Bodies* recognizes that we are all God's children—loved and redeemed. We are each made in the image of God and are thus good and holy. As a faith community, we are called to reclaim this core belief and confirm our understanding that we honor God when we honor the sacredness of our own bodies as well as respecting and honoring the dignity of others' bodies. Sexuality is part of being human and also part of our spiritual selves. It is our hope that *These Are Our Bodies for High School* offers a space for exploring how honoring the body is a shared practice. Young people need guidance and support from their family, friends, and communities to openly affirm and articulate that sexuality is good and part of a holistic understanding of who we are as children of God.

A big goal of *These Are Our Bodies* is the formation of a community of peers and mentors that provides a safe place for participants to honestly and openly engage the content of the program. In the church, when we do our most important work, we often form what are called *covenant groups*. Covenant groups form to help their members deal with difficult topics and grow together.[1] In Genesis, we learn that God formed a covenant with Noah and set the rainbow in the sky as a reminder of that covenant. We hear how God called Abraham to be the father of many nations and worked through Moses to deliver the People of

---

1   This theme of *covenant* not only informs our group ground rules for the program, it encompasses an overarching ethic of love, grace, and compassion at the foundation of the teaching and our lives as faithful people.

Israel to the Promised Land. In the New Testament, Jesus gave us a new promise—that nothing can separate us from God.

> In the New Covenant, Jesus Christ reveals our sexuality as good, refocusing relationships to mutuality, respect, compassion, and hospitality. In the words of the Standing Commission on Liturgy and Music, "Baptism and Eucharist, as sacraments of God's covenant of creating, redeeming, and sustaining love, shapes our lives as Christians in relation to God and to God's creation; this calls us to live with love, compassion, justice, and peace toward all creatures, friend or foe, neighbor or stranger."[2]

As Episcopalians, our Baptismal Covenant[3] guides us in our beliefs as well as our behavior toward neighbor and self. In *These Are Our Bodies*, we see covenants as promises between leaders, parents, and participants as an important part of the program.

In the context of *There Are Our Bodies*, the covenants are between the facilitators, participants, and their adults. We will go over each aspect of the RESPECT[4] covenant:

- R = take RESPONSIBILITY for what you say and feel without blaming others. We want to hear about your experiences and those of the other participants, and we ask that if you are telling about an experience that you leave the names

---

2 Leslie Choplin and Jenny Beaumont. *These Are Our Bodies: Talking Faith & Sexuality at Church & Home, Foundation Book* (New York: Church Publishing, 2016), 14.

3 Book of Common Prayer, 304–305.

4 These "Respectful Communication Guidelines" were developed by Eric H. F. Law and the Kaleidoscope Institute. Versions of this in English, Spanish, French, Korean, and Chinese can be found on their website, along with a further explanation of them. http://www.kscopeinstitute. org/respectful-communication-guidelines/

out of the story, which will protect privacy. We also ask that you keep what the other participants say in this room. We do want youth to share the good things that they are learning, but leave names and other identifiers out of your stories.

- E = use EMPATHETIC listening. This way of listening involves seeking understanding and is built on respect. When we listen empathetically we pay attention to what others are saying, considering especially the emotions involved. We seek to respond in a compassionate way with feeling and insight into their perspective.
- S = be SENSITIVE to differences in communication styles. Each of us feels comfortable communicating in a different way. Some are more reflective and hesitant to disclose thoughts to the group. Some are external processors and like to speak what they are thinking as they think it. We seek to respect the differences in communication styles while encouraging all to participate fully in the way they feel most comfortable.
- P = PONDER what you hear and feel before you speak. We want you to use good listening skills to hear and respond to one another, both lovingly and respectfully. In *These Are Our Bodies*, honesty is important. Everyone will have questions, and the facilitators promise to answer questions honestly. They will give participants the information they need in a way that they can understand. In return, the participants promise to be honest about their questions and their feelings.
- E = EXAMINE your own assumptions and perceptions. In *These Are Our Bodies*, being open is imperative for us to

learn and grow. We want all of you to be open to each other and your facilitators. And we want to be open to the work of the Holy Spirit in and among us.

- C = keep CONFIDENTIALITY. The facilitators promise not to tell the parents what individual participants say or do. We have asked your child that they keep what the other participants say in the room. They may tell you what the entire group did and the facilitators may summarize a discussion to share with the parents. But everyone will keep names and other identifiers private. The facilitators will not tell adults the details of any one participant's sharing. One of the underlying commitments adult volunteers make is to the safety of the youth in our care. When working with youth, leaders might wonder when the promise of confidentiality or privacy should be broken. The safety of the youth or of other people trumps confidentiality. If an adult leader suspects that any youth has been harmed, will be abused, will hurt themselves, or may cause harm to others, the leader should act immediately. Leaders have an obligation to report any suspected abuse or any suspicion that a youth might hurt themselves or others. In the case of suspected abuse or potential harm to themselves or others, leaders will report their concerns to both the clergy at the church and Child Protective Services.[5]

5 The phone numbers for Child Protective Services can be found at https://www.childwelfare. gov/. Mandatory Reporter laws for your state can be found at: https://www.childwelfare.gov/ topics/systemwide/laws-policies/state/.

- T = TRUST ambiguity because we are not here to debate who is right or wrong. Some of the topics we cover will be based on scientific fact. The "T" in respect is referring to the conversations we will have about belief systems and about our theology of sexuality.

The book has nine chapters, one for each session. Youth will use their *Participant Book* during the sessions to reflect on and record what they are thinking, feeling, and learning. You can use this *Parent Book* to follow along with what your teen is covering in each session. You will also find Scripture references to read and contemplate. These can be used on your own, or you may wish to gather with other parents and caregivers while your child is in session for your own discussion and conversations. Within each session you will also find conversation starters for you to use with your family.

At the end of the book (pp. 74–76) are resources of websites and books that you may find helpful to support your learnings and conversations with your child. We highly recommend you obtain a copy of the *These Are Our Bodies: Talking Faith & Sexuality at Church & Home Foundation Book* (New York: Church Publishing, 2016), as it has very pertinent information about all of the topics that will be covered in each of these sessions as well as a comprehensive glossary and resource list.

SESSION 1

OUR
INTRODUCTION

You did not choose me but I chose you. And I appointed you to
go and bear fruit, fruit that will last, so that the Father will
give you whatever you ask him in my name.
I am giving you these commands so that you
may love one another.
—John 15:16–17

Prayer

Almighty God, the fountain of all wisdom: Enlighten by
your Holy Spirit those who teach and those who learn,
that, rejoicing in the knowledge of your truth, they may
worship you and serve you from generation to generation;
through Jesus Christ our Lord, who lives and reigns with
you and the Holy Spirit, one God, forever and ever. *Amen.*[6]

---

6 "Collect for Education," Book of Common Prayer, 261.

Description of this Session

In this session you and your youth will be introduced to *These Are Our Bodies*. You will get an overview of the program. Also, you will have the opportunity to ask questions about what will be covered in subsequent sessions. As part of this you will learn the regular rhythm of the sessions so you know what to expect for your child. During the first session you will begin to consider how sexuality and spirituality intersect.

Scripture Study

Read: Luke 2:41–52 (NRSV)

How This Is Related to Sexuality

For years you've watched your children grow and learn at school, in church, and amongst your family and friends. Sometimes you could control and shape the lessons, sometimes you could not. When they were babies, you may have chosen godparents for them. When they were old enough, you chose their school for them. You picked which shows they could watch and what food they could eat. They are now at an age where they are making more and more decisions on their own. Like letting go of the bike when you were teaching them to ride, are you ready for them to make those decisions? Have you surrounded them with adults you trust and friendships that build them up? If they get lost, will they return to a faith community for answers? There are so many beautiful things about watching your child grow in wisdom and in years; we should all be like Mary and try to treasure as much of it as we can.

Other Bible References

Here are some other pieces of Scripture that might help you think about the importance of the intersection of spirituality and sexuality in a new way:

- Luke 19:45–48—Jesus Throws the Money Changers out of the Temple (the youth discussed this Scripture during the session)
- 1 Timothy 4:11–16—A Good Minister of Jesus Christ
- Ephesians 4:1–16—Unity in the Body of Christ

Personal Reflection Questions

Before you came to this class what did you think about the relationship between sexuality and spirituality?

The opening activity was called "An Interactive Museum." As everyone added their thoughts and ideas to the pages on the wall, you were given a glimpse into others' thoughts, hopes, beliefs, and biases. How did it help you see the variety and diversity of the people and ideas in the room?

Can you take that understanding of others' perspectives out into the world with you? How?

You had an opportunity to listen to other people tell you what they think God has to do with sexuality. Were there any opinions that reinforced your perspective? That made you change your mind or altered your view?

The Bible passage you read told about a time when Jesus was ready for something before his parents thought he was. How has your child surprised you in this way?

How can you prepare to praise your child when they make Christian choices?

How can you prepare to help your child when they make mistakes?

Conversations to Have with Your Family

These are questions you might want to ask yourself now and prepare to discuss with your family. They will help you and your youth to deepen your understanding and commitments. They will also help reinforce the fact that you are your child's best advocate and can be their first stop when seeking information.

- Why is it important that our family participate in *These Are Our Bodies*?
- How did your parents (your child's grandparents) teach you about sexuality?
- How will you respond when your child(ren) ask you about sexuality and spirituality?
- Tell your child the story of a time when you were proud of a decision they made.
- Tell the story about how you chose your child's godparents.

Worship

Leader: The Lord be with you.
Participants: And also with you.
Leader: Let us pray.

From Psalm 139
O Lord, you have searched me and known me.
You know when I sit down and when I rise up;
    you discern my thoughts from far away.
You search out my path and my lying down,
    and are acquainted with all my ways.
Even before a word is on my tongue,
    O Lord, you know it completely.
You hem me in, behind and before,
    and lay your hand upon me.
Such knowledge is too wonderful for me;
    it is so high that I cannot attain it.

A Reading from Romans 12:2
Do not be conformed to this world, but be transformed by the renewing of your minds, so that you may discern what is the will of God—what is good and acceptable and perfect.

A period of silence may follow.

Prayers may be offered for ourselves and others.

The Lord's Prayer

Our Father, who art in heaven,
hallowed be thy Name,
thy kingdom come,
thy will be done,
on earth as it is in heaven.
Give us this day our daily bread.
And forgive us our trespasses,
as we forgive those
who trespass against us.
And lead us not into temptation,
but deliver us from evil.
For thine is the kingdom,
and the power, and the glory,
forever and ever. Amen.

The Collect

O God, you made us in your own image and redeemed us through Jesus your Son: Look with compassion on the whole human family; take away the arrogance and hatred which infect our hearts; break down the walls that separate us; unite us in bonds of love; and work through our struggle and confusion to accomplish your purposes on earth; that, in your good time, all nations and races may serve you in harmony around your heavenly throne; through Jesus Christ our Lord. *Amen.*[7]

....

7 A Prayer "For the Human Family," Book of Common Prayer, 815.

OUR LANGUAGE

Desire without knowledge is not good, and one
who moves too hurriedly misses the way.
—Proverbs 19:2

Description of this Session

In the second lesson, your youth will learn some vocabulary about sexuality. But first we want to know what kind of words they use or know already. They will work on building a common vocabulary so that everyone is on the same page during our conversations and can fully comprehend what others are saying. Hopefully, by naming both the clinical terminology and the slang we will ease some of their anxiety and reduce the stigma of talking openly about sexuality.

In this session your youth:

- Broke into small groups and brainstormed a list of vocabulary terms, both clinical and slang, having to do with sex and sexuality. Then, they came together as a large group to combine these lists into one shared list. From this large list, they determined what sort of language we will use for the rest of our time together.
- Discussed the activity and followed up with a Bible study. Here are some of the questions we asked:
  - Why do you think we feel more comfortable using certain words over others when it comes to sexuality?
  - Why do you think people tend to use metaphor when they talk about sexuality?
  - What does using respectful and accurate language have to do with being a Christian?
  - How do the words we choose as our common vocabulary "build up" those we are in relationship with?

Scripture Study

Read: Ephesians 4:25–32 (NRSV)

How This Is Related to Sexuality

When we were younger we would say, "Sticks and stones may break my bones but words will never hurt me." How much do we wish that were still true today? Words said in anger or with malice can cause wounds much worse than a broken bone. In this reading, Paul isn't telling us we can never get angry, but he is reminding us that we can express all of our emotions in ways that build up instead of tear down.

In a similar way, vocabulary around sexuality can be shocking for some people, especially out of context. That's why words related to sex make such great insults. If we are to "be kind to one another," we can work to use words correctly and gently correct those around us to do the same. We are also able to know each other more fully when we are specific and particular in our language use.

Other Bible References

Here are some other pieces of Scripture that might help you think about the importance of the way we use language in a new way:
- Matthew 18:15–20—Reproving Another Who Sins
- John 1:1–5—The Word Became Flesh

Personal Reflection or Parent Group Discussion Questions

What words or phrases come to mind when you think about sexuality?

What words do your family use when referring to body parts and sexuality? Are they the same words you used when potty training and teaching your child(ren) about their bodies? How have the words you use changed over the years?

When you talk with your child about the body and sexuality do you use clinical terms or metaphor? How do you think this affects the way your child thinks about the body?

What new words do you need to learn to have conversations with your child(ren) about sexuality? What do you do when your child uses a slang word you haven't heard before? Does your family have a safe space for admitting you don't know something?

Do you remember the first time your child used a "bad word" in front of you? How did you react? Would you change anything about how you reacted? How can you use that knowledge to shape how you talk with your child about sexuality in the future?

How might the tone of your voice and your body language shape what your child(ren) share with you? How can you be open to talking with your child about difficult subjects without appearing to judge or criticize their choices?

How can your conversations about sexuality be grounded in faith?

Conversations to Have with Your Family

These are questions you might want to ask yourself now and prepare to discuss with your family. They will help you and your youth to deepen their understanding and commitments. They will also help reinforce the fact that you are your child's best advocate and can be their first stop when seeking information.

- What words do we use as a family to describe our bodies? What about sexuality?
- How do I model a healthy body image, self-esteem, and relationship with my own sexuality for my child?
- How does our family decide and enforce what proper language is?
- Tell a story about a time you were offended by the way someone else described your body or sexuality.
- Tell a story about a time you felt truly seen by the way someone else described your body or sexuality.

OUR
VALUE SYSTEM

Finally, beloved, whatever is true, whatever is honorable,
whatever is just, whatever is pure, whatever is pleasing,
whatever is commendable, if there is any excellence
and if there is anything worthy of praise,
think about these things.
—Philippians 4:8

Description of this Session

In Session 3 the youth will talk about where and from whom they learn values. We receive messages about what is right and wrong or good and bad from many sources. In this session the youth will work to claim their own values by thinking critically about what they actually believe to be good or bad, right or wrong. When your values are well defined it makes making decisions about your sexuality much clearer and easier.

In this session your youth:

- Did an activity about how we develop our value systems and who or what teaches us what is right and wrong or good and bad. We illustrated what value systems different influences (ourselves, caregivers, friends, God, media) in our life have around specific issues regarding sexuality.

- Discussed the activity and followed up with a Bible study. Here are some of the questions we asked:
  - Why do we believe the things we believe?
  - How does our environment impact what we believe and the values we hold?
  - How do our experiences impact our value systems?
  - How have the things we were taught as children influenced the way we behave?
  - How do you decide right from wrong?
  - How do our values inform our actions?
  - How do you think people have determined what is the "law of God"? How might this have changed over time?
  - Do you think that you have to have a certain set of values in order to be a Christian?
  - What would you name as Christian values?

Scripture Study

Read: Romans 7:14–25 (NRSV)

How This Is Related to Sexuality

Temptation is everywhere. David fell prey to it. Jesus wrestled with it. And here, Paul struggles with it. We are taught by our parents, youth ministers, priests, and teachers the choices God wants us to make. Society also tries to influence our decisions and values. How do we discern for ourselves what is right? How do you trust your gut? How do you know what God wants for you? Is it possible to live a holy life, in communion with God, and also be a sexual being? How can you embody your sexuality, and your whole self, in a way that glorifies who God made you to be?

Other Bible References

Here are some other pieces of Scripture that might help you think about personal and cultural values in a new way:

- 2 Samuel 11–12:15—David and Bathsheba and Nathan
- Matthew 4:1–11—Jesus in the Wilderness
- Colossians 3:1–17—The New Life of Christ

Personal Reflection or Parent Group Discussion Questions

When I was a child, I spoke like a child, I thought like a child, I reasoned like a child; when I became an adult, I put an end to childish ways. (1 Corinthians 13:11)

What age do you think you became an adult? When did you begin to intentionally "put an end to childish ways"? In what ways did you change when you made the decision to grow up?

In some ways, you will always see your child(ren) as that tiny toddler who needs your help with everything. How can you enable them grow into independent adults? What age-appropriate responsibilities can you trust them with now? How can you work with them to expand that trust, especially when it comes to decision making?

What do you do when you know your child(ren) has made a mistake and is heading for a difficult time? How do you decide when to step in to help or fix? How do you decide when to stand back and let them learn from failure?

When you know something is wrong and do it anyway, or you know something is right but fail to do it, how does it affect your self-esteem?

What are some of your personal values around sexuality? How have they changed since adolescence? How do you model these values for your children?

What would it take for you to do a better job of matching your actions to your values?

Do you think it's possible for someone to make the right decision all the time? Why?

Conversations to Have with Your Family

These are questions you might want to ask yourself now and prepare to discuss with your family. They will help you and your youth to deepen their understanding and commitments. They will also help reinforce the fact that you are your child's best advocate and can be their first stop when seeking information.

- How have you modeled the values that you want your child to hold?
- How does our family define and live into our value system?
- How does our family hold each other accountable to our values?
- How does our family reconcile when a member makes an unhealthy decision?
- Tell a story about a time when your values and actions did not align; how did you sort this experience out?

OUR IDENTITY

For it was you who formed my inward parts;
you knit me together in my mother's womb.
I praise you, for I am fearfully and wonderfully made.
Wonderful are your works;
that I know very well.
My frame was not hidden from you,
when I was being made in secret,
intricately woven in the depths of the earth.
Your eyes beheld my unformed substance.
In your book were written
all the days that were formed for me,
when none of them as yet existed.
—Psalm 139:13–16

Description of this Session

During this session your youth will explore the multiplicity and complexity of our identities as sexual beings. They will be asked to think about their own identity and orientation. We will talk about what we present on the outside compared to who we actually are on the inside and how we can align these realities.

In this session your youth:

- Spent time creating a personal identity mask. On the inside they wrote their inner characteristics, things that people who are close to them might know but that may not be obvious to the common observer. On the outside they wrote all of the things they think people see when they look at them. We shared our masks with the large group. Then we began to think about our identity in terms of our sexuality, gender, sexual attraction, and romantic attraction.

- Discussed the activity and followed up with a Bible study. Here are some of the questions we asked:
  - Are there things on our inside that we do not want to share with others? Why are we hesitant to share?
  - Are there ways in which you wish you could change the way others perceive you?
  - How can we learn to accept, love, and align both sides of our own masks?
  - How can we see, accept, and love both sides of others' masks, especially when we can't see what they've hidden from us?
  - What can you do to remember that God has given you each aspect of your identity and that each is of equal value?

Scripture Study

Read: 1 Corinthians 12:12–27 (NRSV)

How This Is Related to Sexuality

There are at least two ways to hear this reading. One is to take the almost literal description of your own body. How do all the parts of you—physical, mental, and spiritual—play a part in making up your whole self? Remembering that we are interconnected, as one part of you changes or grows, the other parts are affected. Each part is of equal import and created specially by God. Remember that God loves your whole self even when you don't.

A second way to look at this passage is as if the church is the body and we are all parts within it. We are all connected in the body of Christ. So, even though at times it may feel like that one annoying person you know *has* to be the appendix (utterly useless until it tries to kill you), they, too, are worthy of honor and dignity. God is honored when we lift up the lowly. When we allow everyone to claim the dignity that God has given them, they are better able to live into who God called them to be.

Other Bible References

Here are some other pieces of Scripture that might help you think about identity and orientation in a new way:
- Genesis 25:19—Jacob and Esau
- Genesis 37—Joseph's Coat and His Brothers' Hate
- Matthew 17:1–13—The Transfiguration

Personal Reflection or Parent Group Discussion Questions

In the activity your child(ren) talked about lots of different spectrums: gender, gender expression, sex, sexual attraction, romantic attraction. How familiar with these are you? What additional information do you need? Have you considered how all of these things relate to you?[8]

How would you describe yourself in relation to each identity characteristic . . . ?
- Gender
- Gender expression
- Sex
- Sexual attraction
- Romantic attraction

....

8 You may wish to view the Gender Unicorn, described on pages 50–53 of the *These Are Our Bodies Foundation Book* or at http://www.transstudent.org/gender

Have you discussed your child(ren)'s identity with them? How do you think your child(ren) would describe themselves on each of these measures? What assumptions have you made about your child(ren)'s sexuality?

How do you want to be known by others? How does your child(ren) want to be known?

Thinking back to your adolescence, how did it feel when someone assumed things about you from the outside? How does it feel to continue to experience this?

What did and does it feel like the first time someone really knew you as your authentic self?

What do you do in your life to try to know others more fully?

How does the way you live into your identity honor both yourself and God? How does the way you accept your child's identity honor both them and God?

Conversations to Have with Your Family

These are questions you might want to ask yourself now and prepare to discuss with your family. They will help you and your youth to deepen their understanding and commitments. They will also help reinforce the fact that you are your child's best advocate and can be their first stop when seeking information.

- How can our family be a support system that loves unconditionally?
- How can our family create safe space for accepting others as they are?
- How does our family work toward living an authentic and integrated life?
- How will we create space for dialogue around identity and orientation within our family?

SESSION 5

OUR
SELF-IMAGE

Then God said, "Let us make humankind
in our image, according to our likeness; and let them have
dominion over the fish of the sea, and over
the birds of the air, and over the cattle, and over
all the wild animals of the earth, and over every
creeping thing that creeps upon the earth."
—Genesis 1:26

Description of this Session

In this session the youth will explore the concepts of body and self-image. As we move through the world we learn things about how bodies should be, look, and act. Some of this external narrative may be harmful. Often we internalize these messages, and they become our own internal dialogue. The truth is that we are made in the image of God just as we are meant to be. There is no should. Each body is beautiful and unique. We must teach ourselves self-acceptance and self-love. We must also teach ourselves to accept and love others just as they are because they are also made in God's image.

In this session your youth:

- Created an outline of their body. On the inside of the outline, in pencil, they wrote ways in which their bodies have been or could be described. After discussing, youth wrote over in marker their initial brainstorm the ways in which their body makes them proud.
- Discussed the activity and followed up with a Bible study. Here are some of the questions we asked:
  - What internal narrative about the value of your body presented itself during this activity?
  - Where do you think this narrative comes from; whose voices have you internalized?
  - Have you experienced someone else commenting on your body? What was that experience like?
  - Do you ever find yourself commenting or judging someone else's body? What do you think leads you to do so?
  - When we judge people's bodies or openly comment on them we are eliminating their humanity and reducing them to a set of body parts. How can we remember the whole person we are looking at and honor them as equally beloved children of God?
  - What parts of our society and culture cause you to feel shame about your body and ability?
  - What parts of our society and culture cause you to feel pride about your body and ability?

- ° How might you reframe the narrative you have about your body in a more positive way?
- ° What can others do to promote body positivity for you and for your peers?
- ° In terms of caring for the body, how do you know when to ask for help for yourself or a friend?
- ° What would it take for you to be comfortable in your own skin?
- ° What would it look like for you to live a life free of shame or fear of judgment?
- ° Do you have people in your life around whom you do not feel shame? How did you develop that level of intimacy?

Scripture Study

Read: Genesis 3:1–11 (CEB)

How This Is Related to Sexuality

A lot of small children (2- or 3-year-olds) go through what some parents call a "naked phase," when they never want to wear clothes. Negotiations occur over allowing nudity at certain times and places, almost certainly not when guests are coming for dinner. It's naturally outgrown in a few months, but sometimes it ends abruptly as the child is taught—often unintentionally by a well-meaning adult—that what they are doing is wrong. This is just one example of the many ways we learn what is good or bad, right or wrong, when it comes to our bodies and ourselves.

What does the voice in your head sound like? It may sound like the snake, tempting you into shame and fear, or a parent or adult criticizing something you've done, or a peer commenting on your physical appearance. God offers a gentle, loving voice, asking us, "Who told you that you were naked?" God does not want us to hide ourselves. How can we unlearn the harmful self-image we have internalized?

Other Bible References

Here are some other pieces of Scripture that might help you think about body and self-image in a new way:
- Luke 17:11–19—Jesus Heals Ten Lepers
- Galatians 3:23–29—The Purpose of the Law
- Luke 19:1–10—Jesus and Zacchaeus

Personal Reflection or Parent Group Discussion Questions

Who taught you (either explicitly or implicitly) what your body should be, look, or act like?

How have social expectations of what bodies should look like and how teenagers are supposed to dress changed since you were a teenager? How do you react when someone says something to your child(ren) about their body or their appearance that you disagree with?

What do you love about your body? What do you see in your child(ren)'s body (bodies) that amazes you?

How do you see God's image reflected in your body? How do you see the image of God in your child(ren)'s body?

How do you honor your body? How do you honor your child's body? How have you taught your child(ren) to honor their bodies? What is the difference between honoring someone's body and objectifying them?

How does the way we talk about our bodies honor God's creation within us? Does the way you talk about your body (especially in front of your children) honor God's creation in *you*?

How can we teach our children to respect their bodies (and those of others) without repressing or shaming them?

What does the voice in your head sound like? Is it positive? Does it sound like one of your parents? If you are the voice in your child's head, what are they hearing?

What phrase do they hear the most? What do you want them to hear?

Conversations to Have with Your Family

These are questions you might want to ask yourself now and prepare to discuss with your family. They will help you and your youth to deepen their understanding and commitments. They will also help reinforce the fact that you are your child's best advocate and can be their first stop when seeking information.

- How does our family practice caring for their bodies?
- How does our family's discussion of bodies avoid shame and promote honor?

- How does our family's media consumption promote body positivity and self-esteem?
- How can our family be aware of and prevent eating disorders, self-harm, and other body dysmorphic disorders?
- How does our family reflect God's love in radical self-love?

SESSION 6

OUR
RELATIONSHIPS

So then, putting away falsehood,
let all of us speak the truth to our neighbors,
for we are members of one another.
—Ephesians 4:25

Description of this Session

In this session the youth will explore relationships. They will discuss both the positive and negative dynamics that arise in relationships. They will talk about all types of relationships: friendships, families, and romantic situations. When we (or those we are close to) are in unhealthy relationships, we may not be sure how to create change. When we can name the positive dynamics to look for, we can begin to incorporate them into our own relationships. Relationships take work. Part of being in a relationship is having healthy communication skills. This takes practice.

In this session your youth:

- Thought about different scenarios that might arise in relationships. They acted out these scenarios and then considered both the positive and negative dynamics that emerged. Then, we discussed how healthy communication skills can improve our relationships. Finally, we thought about what we need out of a relationship.

- Discussed the activity and followed up with a Bible study. Here are some of the questions we asked:
  - How would you describe the difference between healthy and unhealthy communication?
  - Share a time that you experienced unhealthy communication. What did you take away from this experience?
  - How would you describe an unhealthy relationship?
  - How would you describe a healthy relationship?
  - How can you work to build healthy relationships in your own life?
  - What do you want and need in a relationship?
  - How do you communicate your needs to those you are in relationships with?
  - How can you be present to the needs of others in your relationships?
  - How can communication affect whether we see things partially or fully?
  - Have you ever experienced what it is like to be fully known by someone? Describe this experience.
  - How do you think God calls us to be in relationship with each other? With ourselves? With God?

Scripture Study

Read: 1 Corinthians 13 (CEB)

How This Is Related to Sexuality

In this passage we hear many descriptions of love. If we believe that God is love and we believe that we are made in the image of God, then we are called to emulate this love. This reading is almost always read at weddings when two people are making their commitment to each other public and permanent. We do so as a reminder to strive to love each other as God loves us. This takes work. When we are in relationship with others we must communicate what we need and what we are capable of giving.

If faith, hope, and love are the three things that remain, how does this frame who you are as a sexual being? There is a mutuality of trust that two people enter into when in relationship. Using this passage as a guide, we can work to be giving and respectful in all of our relationships and are free to expect the same from others.

Other Bible References

Here are some other pieces of Scripture that might help you think about relationships and communication in a new way:

- 1 John 4:7–21—God Is Love
- John 15:12–17—Love One Another

- Acts 2:1–13—The Coming of the Holy Spirit
- Judges 16—Samson and Delilah

Personal Reflection or Parent Group Discussion Questions

In what ways do you think your child is an unhealthy communicator? In what ways do you think you are an unhealthy communicator? What unhealthy communication methods did your child learn from you?

In what ways do you think your child is a healthy communicator? In what ways do you think you are a healthy communicator? What healthy communication methods did your child learn from you?

How do you communicate best? How does your child communicate best?

How can you help your child develop their communication skills?

What other adults do you have in your circle who can help you and your child to communicate consistently and in a healthy manner? How can the church community model good, healthy communication to their children?

How does the love you show in relationships reflect the love God has for you? How can you make this connection more visible for your child?

How is God calling your child to be in relationship to others? How is God calling you to be in relationship to others?

How do the "rules" we express to our children when they get into relationships change the way they communicate with us and with other adults?

How can we recruit other parents to work with us, as a team, to make sure all of our children are in healthy relationships?

Conversations to Have with Your Family

These are questions you might want to ask yourself now and prepare to discuss with your family. They will help you and your youth to deepen their understanding and commitments. They will also help reinforce the fact that you are your child's best advocate and can be their first stop when seeking information.

- Tell your children how you met your partner/spouse/their other parent. How did you navigate the relationship from meeting to defining the relationship to having children?
- What hopes and aspirations do you have for your child's future relationships?
- How much of a role does parental approval play in your child's relationships?
- What would you do if you found yourself in an unhealthy relationship? Who would you turn to?
- How can our family support you when a relationship begins and when a relationship ends?

SESSION 7

OUR
HEALTH

Knowledge is powerful and empowering.
For wisdom will come into your heart,
and knowledge will be pleasant to your soul;
prudence will watch over you;
and understanding will guard you.
—Proverbs 2:10–11

Description of this Session

In this session the youth will gain tools to be able to own and take charge of their own sexual health. There is far too much information regarding sexual health to cover in one session. In this session they will gain more awareness about sexual health. But we will not be able to teach them everything they need to know. You and your youth should seek out more information in a way that you see fit, whether through school, your doctor, or a trusted website.

In this session your youth:

- Went through a series of statements regarding sexual health and determined whether the information provided was true or false. These statements covered most sexually transmitted diseases and infections as well as forms of contraception and terms regarding sex and conception. Then we played a game where they had to consider who they would talk to if they needed help or advice.
- Discussed the activity and followed up with a Bible study. Here are some of the questions we asked:
  - From whom or where did you learn most of what you know about sex?
  - Is there someone else in your life you'd talk to other than the four options we provided? How do you know whom to trust when it comes to talking about sex?
  - What would make you more comfortable when talking about sex?
  - Is there a way to take what you learn in a standard sex education class (the biology and science of how sex works, including birth control and possible infections) and apply your spiritual principles to it?
  - What would it look like for you to align your knowledge of sex and sexual health with your spirituality?

Scripture Study

Read: Matthew 13:10–17 (NRSV)

How This Is Related to Sexuality

Jesus speaks to us in parables that are often confusing and have many layers of meaning. The disciples approach him asking why he teaches in this way. His answer is so that they might understand deeply and fully. In this same way, talking about sexuality is nuanced and complex. But we have eyes to see and ears to listen and so we are tasked with being filled with knowledge. Talking about sex can be awkward and weird. Sometimes talking about sex makes us want to shut our eyes, put our fingers in our ears, and yell, "La-la-la-la, I can't hear you." This is basically what Jesus says people do in the Scripture.

True, some things we will learn by experience. Like figuring out just how spicy is too spicy. But we can use lessons from others to better understand what spicy means before we take a giant bite of that pepper. The adults who care for youth want them to stay safe and to make wise choices. Right now, who do you think would give your child(ren) the best advice that could keep them safe and help them make good choices and who they would really, truly listen to?

Other Bible References

Here are some other pieces of Scripture that might help you think about sexual health in a new way:
- Acts 10:15—Pure and Impure
- Matthew 15:10–20—Things That Defile
- Proverbs 2:10–11—Wisdom Will Guard You

Personal Reflection or Parent Group Discussion Questions

From whom and where did you learn about sexual health? What do you remember most about that experience? From whom and where did your child(ren) learn about sexual health?

Do you know what your child(ren)'s school has taught them about sexual health? Do you feel that the school has told them correct information?

Is there anything you wish they hadn't learned about? How much of the information is or was totally new to you? What other information do you feel they need to have? How do you handle these things?

Whom do you trust to talk to your child about sexual health? How have you communicated to your child and that person that you're okay with them having those kinds of discussions?

Have you talked with your child's pediatrician about the changes in their medical needs as they grow? How can you encourage healthy communication between your child and their primary care physician? When it comes time for your child to meet with their doctor without you, how can you support them in that decision?

What has it looked like for you to align your knowledge of sex and sexual health with your spirituality? What would it look like for your child to align their knowledge of sex and sexual health with their spirituality?

Conversations to Have with Your Family

These are questions you might want to ask yourself now and prepare to discuss with your family. They will help you and your youth to deepen their understanding and commitments. They will also help reinforce the fact that you are your child's best advocate and can be their first stop when seeking information.

- How does our family make sexual health care available (e.g., going to the doctor, birth control, and contraception)?
- How does our family encourage learning about sexuality and sexual health?
- Does our family have rules or internet filters in place that make it difficult to search out answers regarding sexuality?
- Where has our family's sexual education come from up to this point? What needs to be supplemented?

SESSION 8

OUR
DIGNITY

He said to him, "'You shall love the Lord your God
with all your heart, and with all your soul,
and with all your mind.' This is the greatest
and first commandment. And a second is like it:
'You shall love your neighbor as yourself.'"
—Matthew 22:37–39

Description of this Session

In this session the youth will consider how they make decisions
that respect the dignity of every human being. Whether or not we
choose to respect the dignity of others or ourselves applies to
both everyday interactions and important, life-changing events.
We don't have control over how others move through the world,
but we can choose how we respond to them. That being said,
none of us is perfect. We live in a society where respecting dignity

is not an integral part of our culture. Often, we have internalized so much negativity that participating in it becomes habitual. But making a bad choice does not make us bad people. Respecting the dignity of every human being is a lifelong pursuit and we must persist in living into this call.

In this session your youth:

- Explored a variety of scenarios in which they would be called to respect the dignity of others. They were asked to be honest in responding how they might step up, stand still, or step back. Then we debriefed how knowing what is right and doing what is right may or may not coincide.

- Discussed the activity and followed up with a Bible study. Here are some of the questions we asked:
  - What does it feel like when someone does not respect your dignity?
  - How do you deal with realizing what you did was not respecting the dignity of someone else? Yourself?
  - What does consent have to do with the respect of dignity?
  - How do you deal with others who are not respecting dignity?
  - How do you respect the dignity of someone else when they are not respecting your dignity?
  - They say that "hindsight is 20/20," meaning that we almost always know what to do in a situation after it has passed. How can you use your past experiences and this activity to prepare you for the future?
  - How will you account for your dignity when making choices about your sexuality?

Scripture Study

Read: Luke 8:40–56 (NRSV)

How This Is Related to Sexuality

It must have been difficult to come to Jesus for help. The man, Jairus, literally got on his knees to beg for help. The woman was so ashamed of her condition (in addition to the fact that, as a woman, she wouldn't really be allowed to address a man so boldly) she felt the need to sneak her way to healing. Both of these people got what they came for, even though society dictated that they should be treated differently. Is there a chance that Jesus could have stopped his power from healing the woman who touched him in the crowd? Could he have kept walking, carrying her secret as his? Instead, he dignifies her need by praising her bravery and pointing to faith as the cause of her healing.

Jairus's daughter dies before Jesus can get to her. People are told not to trouble Jesus any longer, as if the life of a young girl is too much trouble and not worth the bother. Once again, Jesus commands the narrative by imploring the crowd to simply believe. They had just seen a woman healed simply through the power of touch; why wouldn't his presence be capable of so much more?

In our Baptismal Covenant we are asked, "Will you . . . respect the dignity of every human being?" Our answer is "I will, with God's help." What kind of help do you need from God to be able to stand up for those around you who need defending? We can use kind words, communicate our needs clearly, and hold tight to our values while respecting the dignity of every human being.

Other Bible References

Here are some other pieces of Scripture that might help you think about respecting the dignity of every human being in a new way:
- Luke 7:36–50—A Woman Washes Jesus's Feet
- John 8:1–11—Jesus and the Woman Caught in Adultery
- Matthew 22:37–39—The Greatest Commandment

Personal Reflection or Parent Group Discussion Questions

How do you respect the dignity of others? Specifically, how do you respect the dignity of your child?

How do you respect your own dignity? How do you teach your child to respect your dignity?

How is your child respecting your dignity different from your child respecting you? How can we help differentiate between respect demanded based on authority and the respect we give to everyone simply because they are God's beloved?

How do you respond when someone does not respect your child's dignity? How can you empower your child to stand up for themselves in these situations?

What can we see in Jesus's example of how to respect the dignity of all?

Have you had discussions with your child about when they felt disrespected or hurt? How have you comforted them and helped them use that experience to do better in the future?

Think about when your child first started choosing clothes for themselves. How did you respect the choices they made? How did you help them learn to make appropriate decisions based on where they were going and what they were doing that day? How have your tactics changed now that their bodies are different and the clothes are *very* different?

Can you think of a time when, in hindsight, you may not have been the best parent in the world? How did you recover and learn from that experience? How can we teach our children to use hindsight to become better people and better Christians?

Conversations to Have with Your Family

These are questions you might want to ask yourself now and prepare to discuss with your family. They will help you and your youth to deepen their understanding and commitments. They will also help reinforce the fact that you are your child's best advocate and can be their first stop when seeking information.

- Tell your child the story of their baptism. What do you remember the most about that day? What made it special?
- What will you do when you realize you have made a choice that does not respect the dignity of yourself or others?
- In what ways do we as a family ask for and provide consent? What rules do we have concerning body autonomy?

SESSION 9

OUR THEOLOGY

And when you turn to the right or when
you turn to the left, your ears shall
hear a word behind you, saying,
"This is the way; walk in it."
—Isaiah 30:21

Description of this Session

In this session the youth were given a chance to look back on
what they have learned throughout the different sessions. They
had time individually to reflect on many aspects of their lives
as spiritual sexual beings. They discerned what their guiding
principles are, who or what resources they have to rely on, how
they will make decisions, and more. They were reminded that
they are equipped to bring what they have learned into their
daily life.

In this session your youth:

- Built a personal temple. Using the temple as a model, they described their basic beliefs and driving statements about their theology of sexuality, the people and the places they will turn to as resources or in times of needs, how they will make decisions about their sexuality, what kind of godly sexual human they will be, and what they still need to figure out.
- Discussed the activity and followed up with a Bible study. Here are some of the questions we asked:
  - Did you find creating your own temple easy or difficult?
  - If easy, what would have made it more of a challenge for you?
  - If difficult, what was the hardest part of writing out your temple?
  - What parts of your temple are you most proud of?
  - Are there parts of your temple that feel more aspirational than real to you right now?
  - What can your friends here do to help those things become less hoped for and more everyday real?
  - Have you ever thought you were ready to do something before you actually were? Share that story.
  - Think about when you learned to ride a bike or drive a car (or something similarly skilled). How did you know you were ready to ride without training wheels or without an adult in the car (or do that particular skill unassisted)?
  - How will you know you're ready (to have sex, to be in a relationship, to break up with someone, to get a tattoo, etc.)?

- ◦ How does your trust in God help you to make decisions about your sexuality?
- ◦ "I will do whatever you ask in my name." How can you be a sexual being in God's name?

Scripture Study

Read: John 14:1–14 (CEB)

How This Is Related to Sexuality

This is the last class of *These Are Our Bodies*. Your child may feel a little bit like Thomas, wondering how they can figure out the way forward after all of this. They may feel a little like Philip, needing just that one last (impossible) bit of knowledge before they go. There is only so much that we have been able to cover in the time together. The rest they must figure out with the tools they've acquired. The adults who have spent this time with your children, other trusted adults, the friends made in these classes, peers, the internet can all help with continued learning.

You are not alone in your worries. You are not the first parent to face these challenges. Help is all around if you know who to ask and where to look. God has given you a great crowd of help ready to lift you up and show you the way. God is always with you.

Other Bible References

Here are some other pieces of Scripture that might help you think about your sexuality when you are ready or your theology of sexuality in a new way:

- Hebrews 12:1—A great cloud of witnesses
- 1 Kings 3:5–14—Solomon asks for wisdom
- Song of Solomon 2:7—Do not awaken love until it is ready
- Isaiah 30:21—God will show you the way

Personal Reflection or Parent Group Discussion Questions

What is the greatest takeaway you have from this program?

How is God present with your child in their sexuality? How is God present with you in your sexuality?

What is your theology of sexuality? How does this line up with your child's theology of sexuality? In what ways might they differ?

How will you help your child claim their rightful place as a sexual spiritual being? How will you claim your rightful place as a sexual spiritual being?

After this program is over, how will you seek answers to your questions? How will you assist your child in answering their questions?

Conversations to Have with Your Family

These are questions you might want to ask yourself now and prepare to discuss with your family. They will help you and your youth to deepen their understanding and commitments. They will also help reinforce the fact that you are your child's best advocate and can be their first stop when seeking information.

- What are the greatest things our family has learned in our discussions of this class?
- How will we use what you learned to help others?
- How will we maintain an open dialogue about sexuality in our family?
- Is there anything else you want your child to know about sexuality and spirituality and how they are connected?

RESOURCES

Authors' note to parents:

These Are Our Bodies (Foundation Book) has an extensive glossary, bibliography, and overview of adolescent development that we recommend for your own information as well as to support and understand your child. Your teen's *Participant Book* includes additional terms; you may find it helpful to review this with your child in order to better understand the terms they are discussing.

Organizations

- **The Center for Lesbian & Gay Studies in Religion and Ministry:** Has a mission to advance the well-being of lesbian, gay, bisexual, queer, and transgender people and to transform faith communities and the wider society by taking a leading role in shaping a new public discourse on religion, gender identity, and sexuality through education, research, community building, and advocacy. http://clgs.org
- **The Coalition for Positive Sexuality:** Offers information in English and Spanish for young people who are sexually active or considering sexual activity. http://positive.org

- **Common Sense Media**: A trusted media education resource offers questions and answers regarding privacy and the internet. www.commonsensemedia .org/privacy-and-internet-safety
- **Faith Trust Institute**: A national, multifaith, multicultural training and education organization that works to end sexual and domestic violence. www.faithtrustinstitute.org
- **Integrity USA**: An organization "proclaiming God's inclusive love in and through the Episcopal Church since 1975." www.integrityusa.org
- **Religious Institute**: A multifaith organization dedicated to advocating for sexual health, education, and justice in faith communities and societies. www .religiousinstitute.org
- **Stop Bullying**: Information, videos, lessons, and more to respond to bullying. www.stopbullying.gov
- **Trans Student Educational Resources**: A youth-led organization dedicated to creating a more trans-friendly education system. Their mission is to educate the public and teach trans activists how to be effective organizers. www.transstudent.org

Print Resources
- Berman, Laura. *Talking to Your Kids About Sex: Turning "The Talk" into a Conversation for Life*. New York: DK Publishing, 2009.
- Brill, Stephanie, and Rachel Pepper. *The Transgender Child: A Handbook for Families and Professionals*. San Francisco, CA: Cleis Press, Inc., 2008.

- Dykstra, Robert C., Allan Hugh Cole Jr., and Donald Capps. *Losers, Loners, and Rebels: The Spiritual Struggles of Boys*. Louisville: Westminster John Knox Press, 2007.
- ———. *The Faith and Friendship of Teenage Boys*. Louisville: Westminster John Knox Press, 2012.
- Harris, Robie. *It's Not the Stork!: A Book About Girls, Boys, Babies, Bodies, Families and Friends*. Somerville, MA: Candlewick Press, 2008.
- ———. *It's Perfectly Normal: Changing Bodies, Growing Up, Sex, and Sexual Health*. Somerville: MA, Candlewick Press, 2014.
- ———. *It's So Amazing!: A Book About Eggs, Sperm, Birth, Babies, and Families.* Somerville, MA: Candlewick Press, 2014.
- McCleneghan, Bromleigh. *Good Christian Sex: Why Chastity Isn't the Only Option—And Other Things the Bible Says About Sex.* San Francisco: HarperOne, 2016.
- Mercer, Joyce Ann. *GirlTalk/GodTalk: Why Faith Matters to Teenage Girls and Their Parents*. San Francisco: Jossey-Bass, 2008.
- Tigert, Leanne McCall, and Timothy Brown, eds. *Coming Out Young and Faithful*. Cleveland: Pilgrim Press, 2001.
- Valenti, Jessica. *The Purity Myth: How America's Obsession with Virginity Is Hurting Young Women*. Berkeley, CA: Seal Press, 2010.